THE KETCHUP DEAL

KETCHUP

Janice Marriott

illustrated by Daron Parton

CHAPTER 1

Wheee! A big crack ahead. I bend my knees, shoot my board into the air with my back foot, steady it with my front foot. Fly – ing! Yeah! Over the gaping crack and down. Wheels whirring on concrete. Go!

My mission is to find another supermarket. I've never been outside the city before. Guru always told us it was unsafe. But we've nearly used up the food in the last supermarket in town, so now it's OK for one of us to go exploring. And, of course, it has to be ME because I am the greatest skateboarder of the Superskaters. I am ACE!

This is so new to me. Wow! Look at that mountain – just like the one on the Swiss chocolate wrappers. But the sky in that picture's blue. Out here it's sort of yellowy brown. Everywhere around, there's nothing but rock, dead plants, and huge ice lakes that are no good to skate on. I'm sticking to this shattered motorway. Guru says motorways used to connect the cities, and the cities are where the supermarkets are.

I promised not to go further than three days' travel, but now I've found the motorway, I can't resist the buzz of really moving. The massive slabs of broken concrete make skating a breeze. And skating this fast keeps me warm. Out here, it almost feels like the Disaster never happened – except that there aren't a lot of people around, of course.

I keep a lookout for anything moving. Could be other survivors lurking around. Could be packs of wild dogs. I have to see them before they see me – my only protection is speed.

OK, it was crazy to come alone, but no one else can make a skateboard really fly like I can. I have to admit I'm sort of scared.

My supplies are all gone, which is stupid, stupid, stupid! And I still haven't found a supermarket, not even a shop.

Uh-oh – a rock pile. I flip off the board and climb over, then I slap the skateboard down on the broken road, slant my right foot across the nose of the board, and – stop. I hear something in what should be a totally silent landscape. A girl, arms outstretched, growling, springs from behind a fallen motorway exit sign.

My cat Rascal jumps down from his travelling perch on my shoulder and disappears among the rocks. The girl is thrown off guard. I grab her arm, spin her round, and we both come to a sudden stop against a boulder. She has thick brown hair and stripes of red and yellow clay smeared on her face. While I hold her, she kicks the skateboard over the edge of the concrete. I curse. She bites me, and I let go of my grip on her. She kicks me behind my knees. I collapse in front of her.

"You're caught," she says.

CHAPTER 2

Lots of feet in roughly made sandals surround me. I daren't look up. My eye is about five centimetres from a tuft of hair rooted in the strap of one of the biggest sandals. Yuck! I would have put that one back on the shelf and chosen another pair. I've never thought about shoes being made from animal skins before. I stare hard at these ugly sandals, thinking that they could be the last thing I see. Then I'm jerked up.

There are about fifteen of them. They all have painted faces.

I try joking. "Hey, that's a lot of face paint."

They don't laugh. They're all carrying spears, bows and arrows, or sharpened stones.

"Hey," I say. "Am I invited to your fancy dress party, too?"

They tie my hands together with leather straps and then attach a spear across my bound hands so that the spear sticks out on either side of me.

"Hey, why don't you guys just limbo dance around me?" I call. "Or you could spin me round and use me as a wind turbine. I'd generate electricity."

"Shut up!" snaps one of them.

My heart's hammering, but I'm careful not to seem afraid. The girl I saw first is back, holding my skateboard. "Don't lose that," I say, then bite my lip. Dangerous to let them know it's important to me.

"Go!" barks a fierce-looking guy, and the others push me in front of them. I guess they've all been waiting for him to give an order. That seems pretty strange to me.

We walk – further than I've ever walked before. I'm no good at walking, even without a spear. It seems to me like a totally inefficient way of getting anywhere. We climb over rocks and dead trees. I get dragged some of the way. These guys are strong!

I worry about Rascal. Is he following me? He's never been separated from me before. I'm pushed through dead hanging vines, into a dark, damp cave. I'm scared now. I can hear a dripping sound coming from the back. As my eyes adjust, I see a dark puddle of water.

"Genuine spring water, one hundred percent pure," I say, remembering the label on a bottle in aisle G. No one says anything. I don't think I'm winning hearts and minds with my wit.

They push me around the puddle and up to a slit in the rock wall at the back of the cave. They twist the spear vertical so that I can just squeeze through. Once we're through, they let go of the spear and it springs back to horizontal. We're in a large cave lit with candles that smell like they're past their use-by date. I'm close to panic.

The fierce one comes up close. The rest back off. He doesn't look much older than me, but he acts like he's been bossing people around all his life.

"What's your name?"

"Campbell. Like the soup." They all look mystified. They are so stupid. That's good. I'll have a better chance of escaping.

"Where are you from?"

But I'm not about to tell them about the Superskaters – nine of us munching our way through expired supermarket stock, collecting useful junk and mending electrical appliances.

"Nowhere. I just roam around," I say, staring into his greenish eyes.

They know I'm bluffing. No one could survive the cold wasteland without food and fuel. All I have left in my backpack is a bottle of pop, a packet of instant noodles, matches, my tin mug, and some ketchup. I can eat anything if it's smothered in ketchup.

Fierce One steps back and talks with the others. They offer suggestions, and he barks agreement or rejection. This is so different from our group. It's hard enough just to get us all together for a meeting.

"We can't let him return to his people because they could come and steal our food or take over our cave," some dimwit is saying. I look around and think, "Excuse me, I don't think so," remembering my comfortable bed in the old freezer.

"He could be useful to us," says the girl. "He knows stuff we don't. He travels on wheels." Looks like I've made a good impression. I'll put that down to the deodorant in aisle K.

"Show him our power," says Fierce One.

CHAPTER 3

The candles are snuffed. Many hands spin me around, then feet trip me up, and I fall backwards onto the soft floor. There's light once more, but all I see is a massive bull charging at me. I almost scream, but then I realise I'm looking at the ceiling. Bulls don't charge out of ceilings, even if one could get into the cave. It's a painting – a massive one. When they wave the flaming torch around, the bull looks like it's moving, but it's not. It doesn't scare me now.

They prod me to stand up and spin me again. The horizontal spear is humming. This time I'm staring at a painting of a huge dog, teeth bared, nostrils wide, eyes flickering.

"Tell us where you're from!" yells Fierce One, right next to my ear.

"I'm not telling you anything."

I can tell they're impressed that I'm not cracking easily. I'm impressed myself.

"Leave him in the cave," says Fierce One.

They light two stinking candles on ledges on the wall, then they all leave.

After I don't know how long, the girl comes back carrying a clay bowl. She says, "I'm Fang. We are the Bat Pack."

Since I'm still tied up, she spoon-feeds me. If I wasn't starving, I wouldn't eat this muck. It's like dirty water with lumps in it.

"Soup," she says. She holds a candle over it so that I can see it better.

"Yuck! What's that green stuff?"

"Spinach. It's good. We grow it."

"What do you mean, grow it?" The idea is totally strange. I know kids grow, but food …?

"Well, how do *you* get food?" she asks, as I suck in a spoonful and bits dribble down my cheek. She seems interested – not threatening like Fierce One. I decide I might as well tell her the truth.

"We just graze the shelves. Whenever it suits us."

"Shelves? I don't understand."

"Well, after the Disaster – you know about the Disaster?" She nods. "We found an empty supermarket and made our home there. When it was used up, we found another one."

"Your parents?"

"There's only one alive now – Guru."

"We don't have any."

We are silent, remembering.

"I could brighten up this broth stuff," I say, to change the subject.

"How?"

I tell her to look in my backpack. She disappears, and comes back with the pack and a guy who stands there watching us. She tips everything out of my backpack, and I tell her to open the square packet. She has trouble with the cellophane and finally stabs it with a sharp stick, skinning the block of noodles. She puts them in the broth, doubtfully. Straight away the smell changes to spicy chicken.

"Try some," I say. She shakes her head. So does the guy – Mane, she calls him.

"Spoon some into me, then, will you?"

I eat about half the mixture. I can tell the smell's getting to them both. "Go on!" I encourage them. "Can't be poisoned, can it?"

Fang dips her finger in and licks it. She hands Mane a spoonful. He licks it up, but the noodles wiggle at the corners of his mouth. He spits them out into his hand and examines them. Then he tries again. He ends up spooning great mouthfuls into himself.

"Hey! That's my meal!" I remind them.

"Do you have more of this food?" Mane asks.

"Not here."

"So you've come to steal our food." He sounds angry.

"No! I don't like your food. I was looking for another supermarket."

"Another what?"

"Never mind. Where d'you guys get your food?"

"We hunt, and grow stuff." Hunt? Grow? I don't understand.

"We eat a lot of cats. They're very common."

Cats! Rascal could get eaten by these creeps. I hope he's heading home. I start to tell Fang about Rascal and how he's not for eating, but they don't say anything. They untie me before they leave – not much chance of me escaping from here. Then I'm alone with just one candle.

In the silence, I notice a rustling coming from the back of the cave. I hold the candle up as high as I can towards the ceiling. It seems to be covered with quivering black leaves. Bats! Millions of them. I feel sick. These creatures are scarier than their stupid wall paintings. I lower the candle and try and pretend I haven't seen them.

CHAPTER 4

The night seems to go on for ever in the cave. Finally, after the candle burns out, I fall asleep. Then they're dragging me, covered in bat droppings, out onto a flat stone outside the cave. I see the sun rising, purple and brown like a bruise. Morning. They've tied my hands again, but in front of me this time, and without the spear.

"Ah," I say, "breakfast on the patio."

I'm thinking my fame might have spread before me. I hope they might hail me as the bringer of noodles, but no such luck. They still look grim.

Fang brings a basket full of smooth yellow-green balls and hands me one. "Breakfast," she says.

The others all have them, too. They're actually eating them, tearing pieces off with their teeth.

"What's this?" I ask. I've never seen anything like it.

"Just an apple," Fang tells me, biting into hers. I'm starving, so I do the same. Sweet, delicious juice spurts into my mouth. The flesh is crunchy. I wonder where they got this incredible food. I eat it all, greedily, even the hard bit in the middle.

"Are you a good hunter?" Fang asks.

"I'm pretty good at hunting cockroaches," I joke. They look blank. No sense of humour at all.

"Can you hunt animals? Use a spear?"

"Why would I want to hunt animals? They're dangerous, mostly. Or they steal our food."

They tie me to a dead tree and go off with their spears. After a while, I hear an animal shriek. I hear the Bat Pack yelling. Strange kind of fun, I think. Then they return, dragging a bleeding carcass. With a jolt, I realise: they're going to eat it! I can't believe how different these people are from us.

I watch as they organise themselves into different work crews. Some of them skin the animal (it's a goat, I learn) and cut it into pieces. Others gather fuel and light a fire. Another group skewer the meat on long sticks and hold it over the fire to cook. I'm impressed. We couldn't organise ourselves to show up to a meal at the same time, let alone cook it. But I still gag at the thought of eating a dead goat.

By dusk, the Bat Pack are all sitting around the fire waiting for the cooking to finish. Everyone is singing and drumming. I have to admit, that meat is starting to smell good – like roast-beef flavoured noodles. I've never been hungry before, and I don't like it. If I ever escape from here, I promise myself, I'll never get involved with people who don't snack.

I look up at the sky. It seems to go up and out forever, and stars are starting to appear. We hardly ever see the stars in the city – the sky seems smaller there, and we avoid going out at night. I almost don't mind being held captive by weird people, starving half to death, if I can look at the stars.

Fierce One strides into the circle with a leather bag, which he flings to the ground. Something is moving inside it. I hear a low growling. Rascal!

Fierce One watches my reaction. "See – he'll talk now."

CHAPTER 5

A guy called Horn holds the bag, with Rascal growling inside it, over the fire. The corners of the bag start to smoke. I can't bear it.

"Stop it! What d'you want to know?"

Horn removes the bag slowly and puts it on the ground. Everyone looks at Fierce One.

"How many of you are there?" he asks.

"Nine. We're pretty harmless," I try to laugh, and look at their angry faces. "We fix machines that were made before the Disaster. Machines that cook our food, and give us light and warmth. We're working on machines that will help us travel around. If you let me go, I could get some food for you. And knives."

They are silent for a moment, then Fierce One scoffs, "Food! How can you get us food? You can't even hunt!"

"We have instant food. It's just there for us to take."

They don't believe me. Horn picks up the bag with Rascal in it again. I look at Fang – I thought we'd understood each other last night. She looks away. I almost give up hope.

Then Fang speaks up. "He gave me and Mane some of his food last night," she announces.

"Yeah," I say. "That's what I mean by instant food. I didn't go hunting for that. I just got it from the shelf."

"Where is this instant food?" asks Fierce One.

"All gone. That was the last packet," I mumble. Foolish me, wasting my most valuable piece of barter.

Just then the roast goat is passed around – torn pieces of blackened meat on two big platters.

"Eat," Fierce One says. Fang holds a piece up to my mouth. I'm so hungry I take a bite, but it's disgusting. No salt. Then I have an idea.

"I have some other instant food," I announce. "It makes things taste better. It's in my pack."

Fierce One has lost interest in me, too busy tearing meat off a bone. Fang fetches my pack. I nod my head at the bottle she takes out, but she doesn't know how to open it, and finally puts it into my tied hands. I remove the lid and manage to shake out a dollop of ketchup onto the piece of goat on my knee. I shovel one part goat and four parts ketchup into my mouth. Hmm – not bad!

The Bat Pack are all staring at me. I offer Fang the bottle. "Try some."

Everyone watches while she pours some on her meat like I did, then eats it. She looks at Fierce One. She smiles, a big smile.

"Wow! That's amazing!" she says. Then they all want to try it.

"No!" I yell, just managing to snatch the bottle back. "You can have the ketchup if you give me Rascal."

Fierce One thinks about it for a minute, then opens the bag. Rascal jumps into my lap and settles between my tied arms, eyes like slits, purring. The Bat Pack are impressed by my power over animals. What they don't realise is that my power comes from my skilful use of a tin opener.

Fierce One takes the bottle of ketchup from me. I can tell by the way he looks at the label that he can't read. "I could teach you to read," I say. Guru has made sure everyone can read the labels on tins and packets.

Fierce One ignores this. He pours sauce over his meat and passes the bottle around. Talk gives way to chewing meat and cracking bones. I'm hoping that maybe, now that they know what we have, we can start to talk about trading, or swapping, or sharing – whatever they want to call it. But it isn't that easy.

After a while, Fierce One throws his bones in the fire and then picks up the empty ketchup bottle. He turns to me, pointing at the picture on the label.

"We grow tomatoes like these. We will keep you here, and you can make them into this, this … liquid."

What's he talking about – growing tomatoes? The only tomatoes I know are the ones in tins. "No! I can't *make* ketchup. It's just *there*, in the supermarket. If you let me go, I can get you some, but I can't make any here."

They get angry with me and start arguing. Fierce One interrupts. "Go to this cave of yours and get us some liquid tomato. Two of the Bat Pack will go with you."

I struggle to my feet. This is great. I am going to survive.

"But," he adds, "we will keep your cat hostage till our people return safely." They drive a hard bargain.

CHAPTER 6

We set off next morning. I stroke Rascal and tell him to think of it as a holiday in the country, with fresh meat on the menu every night.

I know the only way I'm going to get my hands untied is by making friends with my escorts – Fang and an older guy called Stew. Away from Fierce One's rules, that should be possible. I just need to find a way to make them like me.

We're walking on a narrow road. I'm tied to them by a long leather rope. I can't walk as fast as them in any case, but I try to walk even slower.

"Can't you go faster?" asks Fang.

"Not without my board," I say, dragging my feet. Fang's carrying the skateboard. "I could show you how to use that thing," I tell her. "You don't have to untie me." She's interested. "Put it down on the road." She does. Stew looks daggers at her, but he's curious, too.

I teach them as we go. Fang has good balance and fast reactions. Stew is suspicious of wheels and prefers to run. I show Fang how to balance on the board and kick it along. She tries to snap the board up a bank of concrete with her feet. She falls, and the board darts away from her. I can't catch it because the leather rope is tight between me and Stew.

"Flip!" she spits. I can see she's getting the bug. She has to scramble off the road and find the board in the frost-covered rocks.

"If you untie me, I'll be able to teach you easier," I point out. "I'm not going to make a run for it. You have the board, and you can both run much faster than me."

They look at each other. I know they're thinking of Fierce One and his orders. Then Stew unties me.

"Thanks." We all pretend that nothing big's happened.

We travel on. Sometimes Fang skates. Sometimes I do. Stew runs. We tell each other stories we've heard about the old life.

"Our old person, Guru, says people could fly like birds."

"One of ours told us that before the Great Disease, people used to live for a long time. They had homes in towers high above the ground."

I laugh. "We think they had control over animals then. We have huge pictures of people with animals, all around our supermarket." I know this will impress these hunters.

"We've never been this far before," Fang says, amazed at all the burnt rock. "We saw purple clouds, and heard about stinking fumes."

"It's cleared now."

"And they said there was no food in the city." I guess she means animals.

"True. Unless you want to eat rats." I grind a kerb and then hand the board to her. She does her first Ollie. She's getting too clever. I take the board back, speed down a slope, bend my knees, leap into the air, flick the front of the board with my toe, turn it into a perfect spiral, land with my feet back on the board, and glide towards them.

"Get that!" I shout.

Stew stares. Fang laughs. I feel we are getting to know each other.

We travel on, sleep a night in an underpass, travel on again. We come to a great spiral of motorway, tilted on its side. Too good an opportunity to miss. I do a one-handed handstand from the raised side of the road, my back like a crescent moon, knees bent, feet nearly touching my head. I feel I'm in the zone. Untouchable. Misery-proof. Fang's impressed, too.

On the fourth day, we reach the outskirts of the ruined city. I could race away from these two on the old motorways. But I don't. We're a group now. I want to show them my place, my tribe. We're going to have one big party!

CHAPTER 7

We enter the supermarket through the roof. I take them down the rope, my usual route.

"Don't be nervous," I tell them. "We're really laid-back here. No rules. Just relax."

We land on the pile of cushions. Home, at last!

Suddenly there's major noise. Alarms, hooters, sirens. Fang and Stew are startled, and I'm shocked. Is this some kind of welcome home act?

Betty and Maxwell ride up on their boards. Great! When they see Fang and Stew, they jump off and raise iron bars above their heads. Not great.

"Hey, gang! It's me!" I expect hugs, laughter, stories. What I get is anger.

"Where've you been? Who are these people?"

"Cool it, guys. I've brought some friends over."

"Have you found a supermarket?"

"No, but I …"

"No strangers allowed. It's a rule."

"What?" I'm stunned. The Superskaters never had rules before. Everyone just does their own thing.

"They're our prisoners now," says Betty.

"No – they're my friends!"

Betty and Maxwell tie Fang and Stew's hands behind their backs with tape. Suddenly the people I've lived with all my life seem sinister, not to be trusted.

Guru zips up on her little speed bike, which completely freaks Stew. "Did you find another supermarket?" she demands. The elder of my group is shaming me with her rudeness.

"No. I didn't," I yell. "But I found some people. They know how to …"

"Take them to the freezer room," Guru orders. Maxwell and Betty put paper bags over Fang's and Stew's heads, and Kenny and Milo appear and lead them away. I can't believe this is happening.

"What's up with you lot?" I hiss. They all start yelling and crying.

"There's no chilli beans left!"

"No bacon and cheese noodles!"

"No raspberry jam!"

"Shut up, you wimps!" I yell. "Get real! The Bat Pack have to go out every day and *kill* their dinner!"

"That's disgusting!" says Maxwell. "You should've kept away from them. Have you forgotten what you went out there for?"

"They're my friends," I shriek. "And they've kept Rascal hostage, so …"

"Some friends," Guru says quietly.

"They just want some ketchup. I bought my freedom with this promise. I can't go back on a deal."

"Ketchup? Are you mad?" shouts Betty.

"You've failed in your mission to find a supermarket," says Guru. "We were relying on you." She swoops her bike around in a circle and takes off down the aisle. Maxwell and Betty scoot behind, without another word to me.

I've never felt so alone. I go to my space, the chest freezer filled with cushions that's been my bed ever since we moved in here. I dreamt about it when I was in that bat-infested cave. But tonight it's a place to plan my next move, not to sleep.

I wait till the middle of the night and then creep along to the big freezer. There's a dim light showing through the air holes that we cut in the door, ages ago. I know there's no door handle on the inside, so the door won't be locked. The only problem is Milo, standing guard. I sneak up behind him, slowly, slowly. I throw my blanket over his head and, while he's struggling, push him into the chiller next to the freezer and slam the door.

"It's only me – Campbell," I whisper through one of the air holes. "I'll let you out later."

Then I open the freezer. Fang and Stew are cowering in a corner.

"The management apologises for the standard of accommodation," I burble, untying them. "We don't usually put our guests in a freezer."

"Freezer?" queries Fang. "It's not that cold in here."

"No. It's not turned on. We only keep one of the freezers going, to make ice for drinks in the summer. No need for more. None of our food rots. We just use them as cupboards. Never been used as a cell before, though." I can't stop talking, I'm so embarrassed. I don't know what to do next.

"What do you mean, you make ice in summer?" asks Stew.

"How can that be?" asks Fang. "Can you keep food frozen, too?"

Are they kidding me? Surely they must know about electricity. I shrug. "Come on. We've got to get you out of here."

We're just about to head off down the aisle when Betty springs into the doorway, followed by Maxwell and Kenny. "Gotcha!" she shouts. Fang and Stew are tied up and imprisoned again, and so am I – by my own people! I can hardly believe it. Then I hear Milo calling for help, and remember it was me that locked him up. The world is suddenly upside down.

We hear them releasing Milo from the chiller, and then the sounds of their skateboards as they roll away, leaving us trussed and trapped.

CHAPTER 8

Fang shivers. With my foot, I flick the switch of a small heater that Guru keeps in the freezer.

Stew stares at the heater as the bars start to glow orange. "Is that thing on fire, or what?" he asks. "Is it safe?"

"It's electric power," I say. "It's safe."

"You mean you can make heat as well as cold?" He's not sure whether to believe me.

"Yeah. Long story," I say.

"It's a long night," says Fang.

So we talk. I try to explain about car batteries. "We get an alternator out of a car. It drives the fan belt, which drives the main engine in a car, right?" They look blank. "So, what we do is use the alternator and mount a propeller on it, see?" They don't see.

"The wind turns the alternator, and it produces 12 volts direct current. You know what volts are?"

"No."

I'm not so sure I know, either. Our knowledge has lots of holes in it.

It's clear Stew hasn't taken in a word I've said. He pulls a leaf out of his pocket and unwraps it carefully. I'm thinking he must have collected some straight nails (valuable) or ball bearings (very valuable). He shows me a little pile of tiny grains, like the pips in raspberry jam. I laugh at his treasure. Stew tells me they are seeds. "I gather them everywhere I go," he says. "We plant every kind of seed we find, in case it grows into something we can eat."

"Grows?"

Fang and Stew look at each other. They think I'm an idiot.

Fang tells me how stupid she thinks we Skaters are, which I don't want to hear. She explains how the Bat Pack use heated stones from the fire to keep their seedbeds warm. She reckons that with our heat we can grow food, and with cold we can store it through the summer. I don't understand. I'm picturing bottles of ketchup growing in front of a heater. "It's you lot who are stupid," I mumble.

Stew says, "In exchange for your heat machine, we could show you how to grow food. Bring you goats and cats for meat."

Fang stamps on Stew's foot with her heavy sandal. "Not *cats*," she hisses. "Rats, that's what we mean."

"Rats?"

"Dead ones. To eat."

We're all silent. These are very new ideas.

Then the entrance alarm bells ring. We can hear a voice, shouting through the aisles.

"Where are my people? Release them. You are surrounded."

It's Fierce One.

CHAPTER 9

Through the holes in the door, we can see Bat Packers rushing around, following Fierce One's orders. Sleepy Skaters appear, dragged from their nests by the commotion. Guru lets us out of our cell, and we're untied. Fierce One roars at Fang, "Did you think I wouldn't follow you? I won't let my Pack go unprotected into the unknown." He glares at Guru. "When they don't come out with that liquid tomato, I act."

Guru stares at him, then she smiles. "Welcome," she says. I can't believe it. "We can't give you unlimited ketchup," she continues, "but we can give you some."

"In return for Rascal," I yell. "That was the deal."

Fierce One lays a bag on the ground. I know from the yowling that it contains Rascal.

Fierce One booms, "In exchange for this cat, we want ..."

"Control over heat and cold!" demands Fang. "*And* some ketchup."

Fierce One is surprised by Fang's interruption, and in that moment of silence, Guru says calmly, "I think we should talk, don't you? In the sunroom, perhaps?"

Everyone, Skater or Packer, is so freaked out from seeing more strangers than they've ever seen before that they agree, and we all stumble and ride along the corridor and through the supermarket. The Packers don't like the big posters of smiling chefs with meat cleavers in their hands and the pizza woman about to throw a Super Supreme.

In the sunroom, horizontal rays of the rising sun stream in through our greatest treasure, the one unbroken window in the supermarket. The Packers gasp in amazement. Fierce One puts down the Rascal bag on his side of the room. Maxwell runs to aisle G and gets the ten remaining bottles of ketchup and puts them on the opposite side of the room. I think the Pack are expecting us to be organised and talk in turns – maybe have some sort of ceremony. Instead, each of us just turns to the Packer nearest us, and we talk, one to one. That's what Skaters do best.

Kenny asks Fierce One, "Got any wheels, batteries, timber, stuff like that?"

"No."

"Dead loss, then."

Betty explains electricity to Stew and Horn. "I use the alternator to charge a battery, then a series of 12-volt batteries, all hooked up. Off that we run the lights. There's plenty of wire around."

Maxwell adds, "We got an inverter from a place around here that's full of stuff like that. It changes 12 volts to 110 volts – so we can run electrical appliances."

"Hi-fi's, microwaves, popcorn machines!" shouts little Kenny.

Guru says to Fierce One, "We realise we've been living a non-sustainable lifestyle."

"I think she means the food's running out," says Milo.

"What if we traded?" Guru suggests. "You could provide us with food. We could give you power." I remember the soup they fed me in Batland, and I'm not very thrilled. Then I remember the apples.

"Campbell could work out a skateboard route between us," says Fang. That sounds more like it.

"What d'you say to a skateboard in exchange for some of those apples?" I ask her.

"We can bring you apples, and meat, and vegetables, if you bring us a freezer that makes meat cold in the summer," says Fierce One.

"Strange thing to want," says Kenny.

"We could set up batteries to produce a current that will be inverted to 110 volts, which will run a freezer for you," says Maxwell.

Fang cuts him short. "Don't talk that jargon at us. Just say if you will or not."

"We'll try," says Guru.

Guru and Fierce One start working out how to turn the sunroom into a plant-growing room.

"We Packers will vote on which one of us stays and teaches you how to grow vegetables," says Fierce One.

"What's voting?" I ask.

Stew and Fang look at each other with eyebrows raised. I glare at them. Betty, playing the peacemaker, says, "I think we all have a lot to learn."

The meeting's beginning to fall apart. Kenny is starting to fiddle with a hinge he's holding. Sunmaid wants to get back to rebuilding skateboards. I retire to my cushioned freezer, my think-tank, to work out how we'll get a freezer up to Batland. I'm working on an idea using supermarket trolleys, improving the road with planks and rock causeways as we go. Rascal leaps in with me and curls up under my chin, as though nothing unusual has happened. I stroke him and promise him the last of the tuna. Everything's going to be fine.

Then Fierce One is there, glowering over the edge of my freezer, peering down at me.

"I looked after that cat well," he declares. "And I want you to teach me how to walk on wheels."

Hmm. The future will be interesting.